STEPHEN CURRY

and the

NBA ALL-STARS

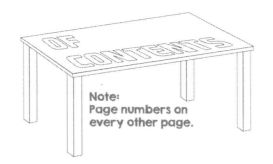

Note:
Page numbers on
every other page.

NBA PLAYERS

NBA PLAYERS

ALL-NBA 3rd Team

2015-2016

LaMarcus Aldridge

2015-16 Season Stats

PTS 18   REB 8.5   AST 1.5

Paul George

2015-16 Season Stats

PTS **23.1** REB **7** AST **4.1**

ALL-NBA 2nd Team

2015-2016

Chris Paul

2015-16 Season Stats

PTS **19.5** REB **4.2** AST **10**

Damian Lillard

2015-16 Season Stats

| PTS | 25.1 | REB | 4 | AST | 6.8 |

2015-16 Season Stats

PTS **28.2** REB **8.2** AST **5**

ALL-NBA 1st Team

2015-2016

Kawhi Leonard

2015-16 Season Stats

PTS **21.2** REB **6.8** AST **2.6**

15

Lebron James

DeAndre Jordan

2015-16 Season Stats

PTS **12.7** REB **13.8** AST **1.2**

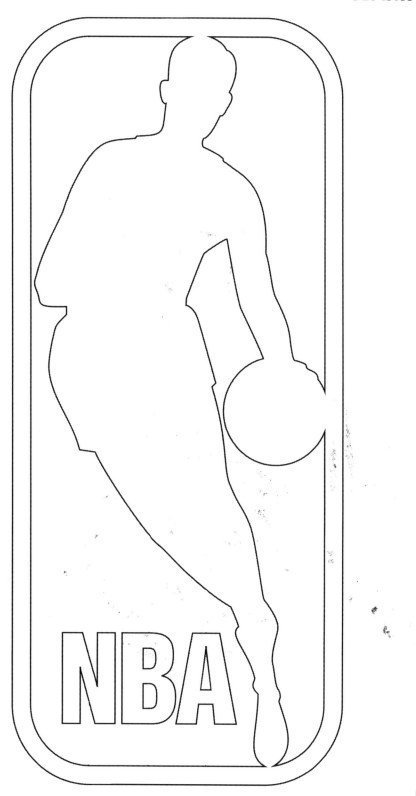

20

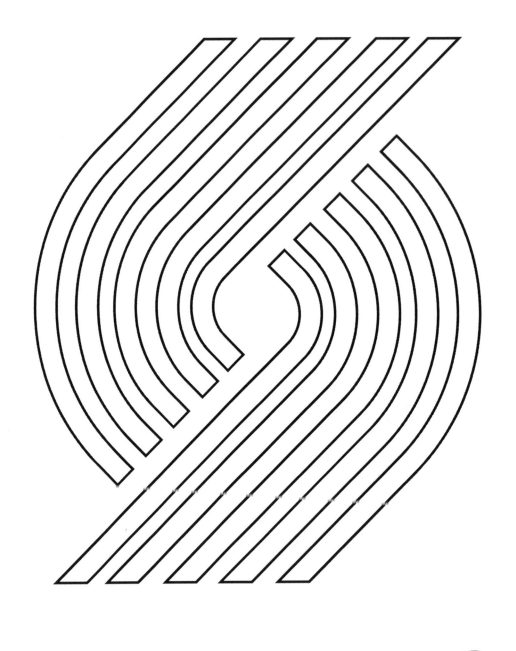

CHARLOTTE BOBCATS

21

22

23

24

27

28

29

30

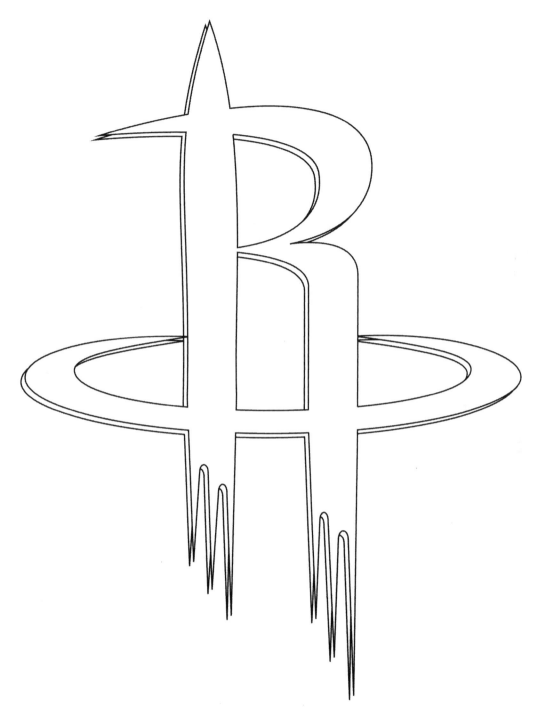

HOUSTON ROCKETS

32

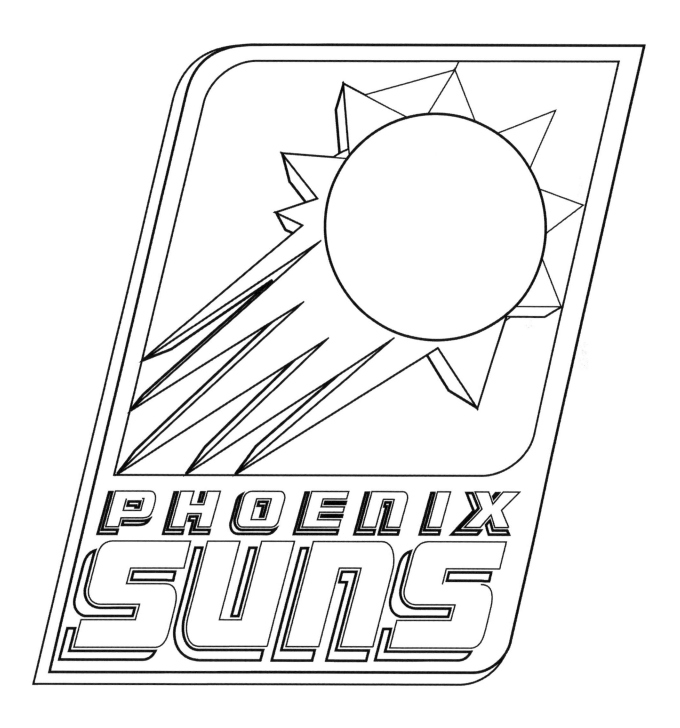

33

WIZARDS

DESIGN A PLAYER!

37

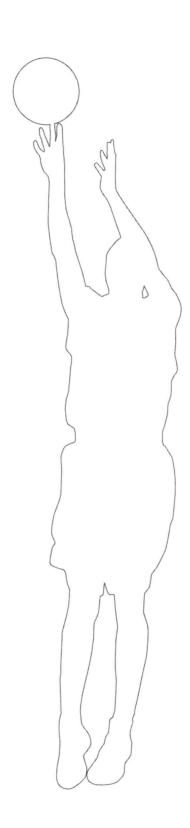

38

DESIGN A SHOE!

40

DESIGN A JERSEY!

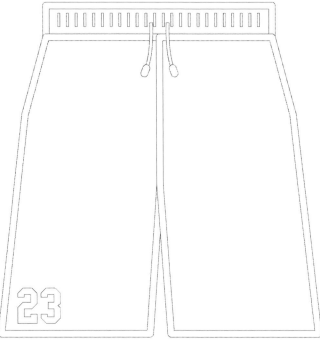

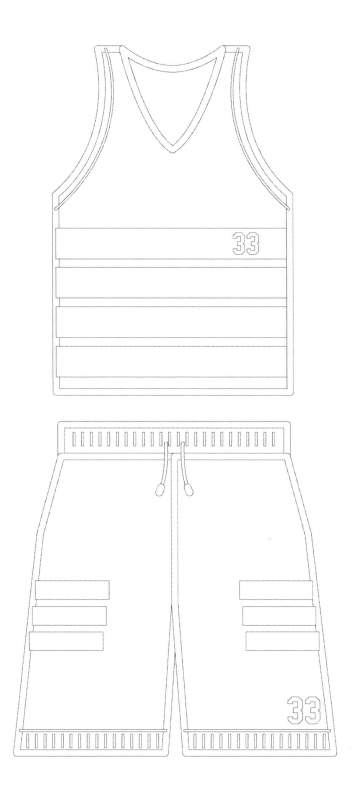

42

43

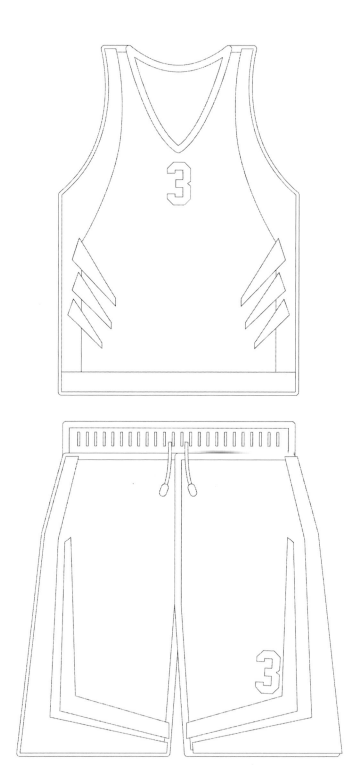

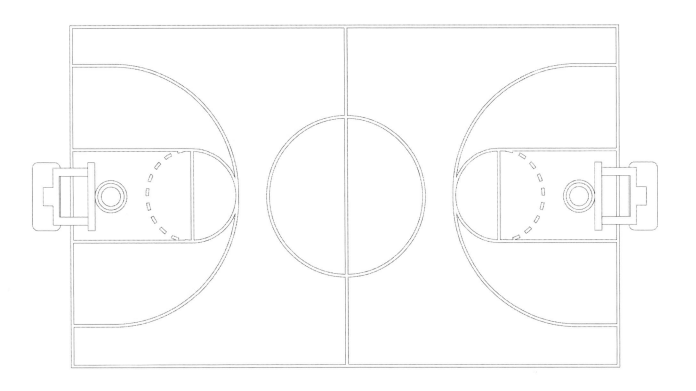

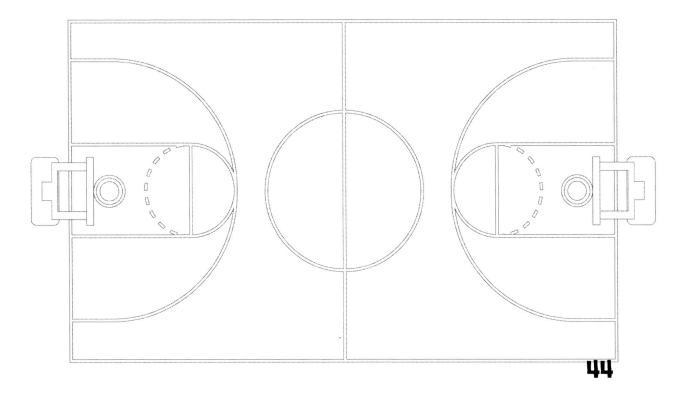

44

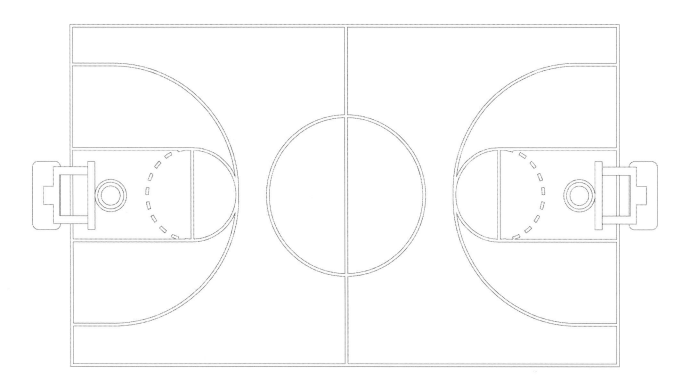

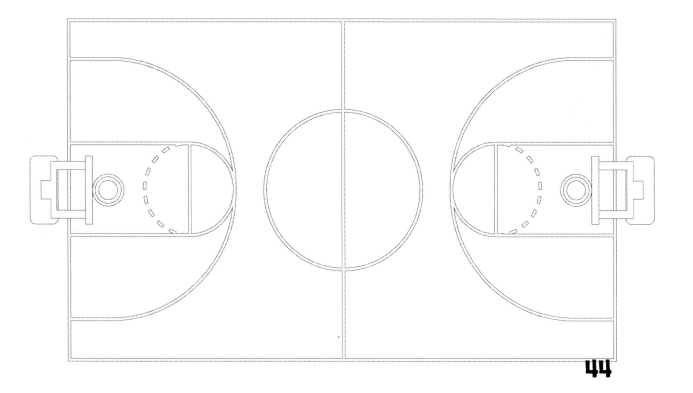

45

BONUS PLAYER

Carmelo Anthony

2015-16 Season Stats

PTS	REB	AST
21.8	7.7	4.2

NEW YORK

7

BONUS PLAYER

James Harden

2015-16 Season Stats

PTS 29 **REB** 6.1 **AST** 7.5

BONUS PLAYER

Derrick Rose

2015-16 Season Stats

PTS **16.4** REB **3.4** AST **4.7**

BONUS PLAYER

James Harden

2015-16 Season Stats

PTS	REB	AST
29	6.1	7.5

BONUS PLAYER

Derrick Rose

2015-16 Season Stats

| PTS | 16.4 | REB | 3.4 | AST | 4.7 |

BONUS PLAYER

Dwayne Wade

2015-16 Season Stats

PTS	REB	AST
19	4.1	4.6

BONUS PLAYER

Dwayne Wade

2015-16 Season Stats

PTS	REB	AST
19	4.1	4.6

Made in the USA
San Bernardino, CA
06 April 2017